100 YEARS OF FABIAN SOCIALISM 1884-1984 ·

he Fabians' self-
age extended to their
orks. The window
dered by Shaw in
10, and designed by
roline Townshend,
as an exercise in the
ock medieval. (The
iginal was stolen by a
ief who believed it to
e ancient stained
ass). Shaw, Webb and
ease, the first
cretary of the
ciety, are depicted
-moulding the world,
der a coat of arms
nich celebrated their
litical "permeation"
th a wolf in sheep's
othing. Beneath, at a
rine of Fabian plays
d reports, are the
ecutive. H G Wells
xtreme left) thumbs
s nose at his elders,
ho were outraged by
s free lifestyle. The
hers are (left to right)
harles Charrington,
ylmer Maude,
R Stirling Taylor,
wson Dodd, Mrs
ember Reeves, Mary
ankinson, Mabel
ckinson, Mrs Boyd
awson, Caroline
ownshend (creator of
e window).

· CONTENTS ·

Edited and co-ordinated for the Fabian Society
by Deirdre Terrins and Phillip Whitehead

© Fabian Society March 1984

Designed by Tamasin Cole

Produced by G&B Arts Ltd., London N16 (100% TU)

Published by **The Fabian Society**
11 Dartmouth Street
London SW1H 9BN

ISBN 0 7163 4012 7

• INTRODUCTION •

A lecture at the Fabian Society, Essex Hall: 'a question from the rear'. Hugh Thompson in Scribner's Monthly 1892

The Fabians are the oldest socialist society in Britain. The founding Fabians took their name from the Roman general Quintus Fabius, known as Cunctator from his strategy of delaying until the right moment the main thrust of his attack. The early Society tried to express this with the symbol of a tortoise and the slogan "when I strike, I strike hard."

The first Fabians, who had been meeting in 1883 as the Fellowship of the New Life, hit upon their new name at a meeting on 4 January 1884 in the London home of **Edward Pease**, a young solicitor. They were earnest, romantic and middle class — characteristics not uncommon in the Society over the next century. Their aim was "to help in the reconstruction of society in accordance with the highest moral possibilities".

In the Fabian Essays of 1889, the contributors' diverse viewpoints expressed an early characteristic of the Society which it has never lost — freedom from any imposed 'line' to which all must adhere. Only the author of a particular publication or policy bore the responsibility for it.

Their views, associated with names as influential as **G B Shaw**, the **Webbs**, **Graham Wallas**, **H G Wells** and in a later generation **R H Tawney**, **Leonard Woolf** and the **Coles**, carried Fabian influence into fields as diverse as local government and literature, academia and the colonies, and to the writing of the Labour Party constitition itself.

It was this which made the early Society a deep reservoir of talent for the emerging socialist movement, long before it became a think-tank for the modern Labour Party. It consists of socialists, but it has avoided capture by any one received version of socialist truth. The early Fabians believed in 'permeation' of institutions by social reformist ideas, patiently setting out a rational case for change and improvement which the thinking citizen would, over time, embrace. The "inevitability of gradualness" was the philosophy of missionary educators, wedded to reform rather than revolution, through collectivist solutions which they believed they could urge upon reforming governments. It was an influence which they sought to exercise principally (but not exclusively) through the Labour Party. From their first tract up to their hundredth year the distinctive features of the Fabian contribution have been its range, its relish for ideas, and its belief that the exposition of argument rather than the explosion of anger would bring the socialist commonwealth closer.

By 1945 229 Labour MPs were Fabians, and the modern Society has been enriched by the work of **Tony Crosland**, **Richard Titmuss**, **Peter Townsend**, **Brian Abel-Smith** and **Tony Benn**.

The first Fabians of 1884 would still be recognisable at a Fabian gathering today. They for their part would find it hard to understand the present society in the complex world of modern mass democracy. But in understanding they would also approve. The process of rational persuasion goes on.

FOUNDATIONS

> We talked revolution, anarchism, labour notes *versus* pass-books, and all the rest of it, on the tacit assumption that the object of our campaign, with its catchwords, 'EDUCATE, AGITATE, ORGANISE' was to bring about a tremendous smash-up of existing society, to be succeeded by complete Socialism. And this meant that we had no true practical understanding either of existing society or Socialism. Without being quite definitely aware of this, we yet felt it to a certain extent all along; for it was at this period that we contracted the invaluable habit of freely laughing at ourselves which has always distinguished us, and which has saved us from becoming hampered by the gushing enthusiasts who mistake their own emotions for public movements.
>
> **G B Shaw** *A Short History of the Fabian Society* 1892

Signatures of first Fabian essayists

Edward Pease — the first Fabian

At an early Fabian meeting a remarkable new recruit, enlisted to take the minutes, wrote immodestly that it "had been made memorable for the first appearance of **Bernard Shaw**". The Fabians were lucky in the hour of their birth. The temper of the time attracted to them a wide range of talents then, as Shaw put it, "ripening for the work that lay before us." The 1880s and 1890s saw an upsurge in socialist activity in Britain, with **Keir Hardie**'s ILP, **Hyndman**'s Social Democratic Federation and the Socialist League of **William Morris**. The economic depression of the 1870s and the resultant heavy unemployment, linked with the rigours of the Poor Law, worsened the lot of the working class. In the 1880s the researches of **Charles Booth** into poverty in London revealed that 30% of the population of the richest city in the world lived on or below the poverty line. The Fabians went straight to the point in their first tract. It was headed *"Why are the Many Poor?"*

The Match Girls' Strike and the 1889 London Dock Strike were the background to the *Fabian Essays* (1889), written "with a common conviction of the necessity of vesting the organisation of industry and the material production in a State identified with the whole people by complete Democracy".

The essayists included Shaw, the man of letters, **Sidney Webb** the civil servant, **Graham Wallas** the educator, **Sydney Olivier** the future enlightened imperialist, and **Annie Besant**, who had led the Match Girls' Strike. A thousand copies were sold within the month, and *Fabian Essays* was subsequently reprinted at 25,000 per annum. They were edited by Shaw, and were aimed at redressing the gross inequalities of society, with an alternative organisation of industry, the taxing of rents, and the return to the workers of the fruits of their labour. The Fabians had no time for violent upheaval as an alternative to democratic change. The power of local government, and of trade unions, was to be pressed to this aim.

Annie Besant — liberated socialist

G B Shaw himself, playwright, critic, and pamphleteer, at his most serious when he was most flippant, now began a 65-year association with the Fabians. His literary output was prodigious. The frequency of revivals of "Widowers Houses", Major Barbara", "Man & Superman", "The Doctor's Dilemma", "John Bull's Other Island" and "On the Rocks", testify to Shaw's ability to illuminate moral problems with wit and ferocity. They still make a contribution to the debate of ideas, as they have done for four generations.

The literary output never prevented political involvement, including service on the St Pancras Vestry and on the Labour Representation Committee which, in 1900, led to the development of the Labour Party itself.

Annie Besant, a woman of powerful emotions and many talents, was already famous for her advocacy of birth control, her oratory and her popular journalism. Before she moved on to other enthusiasms in India, she brought to the Fabians a real link with the new world of trade unions and popular agitation.

G B Shaw — 'a good man fallen among Fabians' V I Lenin

Walter Crane's cover design for the first edition of *Fabian Essays*, published 1889 under the title *Socialism*.

London slums in the year of Fabian Essays 1889

THE WEBBS

The Young Beatrice
Webb, photographed
by Shaw

Beatrice Webb was born in 1858 into a family of successful upper middle class entrepreneurs. She was beautiful, intelligent, but also highly strung. Her childhood, which was lonely and starved of affection, led her to search restlessly for order and certainty. For years she was torn by frustrated love for **Joseph Chamberlain**, knowing that she could not accept the subordination that would come if she agreed to marry him.

Eventually she found happiness in a true partnership of the intellect with someone very different. **Sidney Webb** was an awkward, lower middle class self-educated intellectual, whose brilliant scholastic achievements gained him a place at the Colonial Office.

Their marriage brought them fulfilment. Sidney always adored Beatrice, and she in turn gained an inner peace and self-confidence from his loving affection.

The partnership was also vital to the development of their work. Beatrice provided the imagination and intuitive grasp, Sidney the brilliant analytical powers and clarity of prose. Authors of more than 20 major works, such as *History of Trade Unionism, Industrial Democracy, A Constitution for the Socialist Commonwealth of Great Britain,* and innumerable Fabian pamphlets, their scholarly reputation has remained undimmed.

But they were also practical reformers who helped to change the face of British society.

THE WEBBS

The Webbs' earliest successes were educational. Sidney was the innovatory chairman of the most prestigious education committee of the **London County Council**, the **Technical Education Board**, for 16 years. Together they founded the **London School of Economics** and the **New Statesman**, and helped create Imperial College and reform London University.

With **Lloyd George** and **Beveridge**, Beatrice and Sidney Webb can justly be said to be the founders of the modern Welfare State. In particular, Beatrice's 1909 *Minority Report to the Royal Commission on the Poor Law,* and the Webbs' subsequent Prevention of Destitution campaign, laid down a blueprint for the development of welfare programmes to cater for the disadvantaged.

Intellectuals, educational reformers, propagandists for the Welfare State, the Webbs also played a crucial role in the development of British socialism. Sidney was the chief architect both of the new Labour Party Constitution and the 1918 Election Manifesto. *Labour and the New Social Order* was a clear statement of Webbian objectives — a national minimum wage, democratic control of British industry, and increased municipalisation. More important, it provided the Labour Party, for the first time, with a definite programme for changing society. The Webbs had captured the Labour movement for their ideas and helped prepare the Labour Party for power.

After Sidney's service in two Labour cabinets, the elderly Webbs travelled widely in the Soviet Union and let impression harden into infatuation with what they had seen. They were too old now to shed this last illusion. They should be remembered for their belief that society needed to be changed and that its individualistic and selfish attributes could be transformed into a moral order. Pragmatic, evolutionary, collectivist, their approach was always founded on a deep commitment to a democratic pluralist state.

Sidney Webb

THE WEBB OF DESTINY

MR. SIDNEY WEBB. "I AM WAVING THIS RED FLAG, NOT PROVOCATIVELY, BUT TO SIGNALISE WHAT I HAVE SO HAPPILY CALLED THE 'INEVITABILITY OF GRADUALNESS' WHICH MARKS OUR ROLLER'S ADVANCE".

No, dear, I do not even look at your photograph. It is too hideous, for anything. Do be done in a grey suit by Elliott and Fry and let me have your *head only* — it is the head only that I am marrying!

Beatrice Potter to Sidney Webb on their engagement

SECOND GENERATION

An attraction for
women of spirit

Early in the new century the Fabians took up Mr
H G Wells, who had acquired a mass following with his
science fiction and ability as a popular analyst of the
future. Wells was then in his thirties, bumptious,
irreverent, unable to resist young women of spirit. The
Fabians found him a harsh critic who broke the rules of
private behaviour. He found them timid, and mocked
their inability to expand and to be involved in the parliamentary struggle. Scipio, the hammer of Carthage,
should be their inspiration, Wells said; the Fabians had
permeated English society with their reputed socialism
"about as much as a mouse may be said to permeate a
cat". The 'old guard' did not retreat under this
onslaught. They counter-attacked, and Shaw was brutal
in his turn.

The young Wells

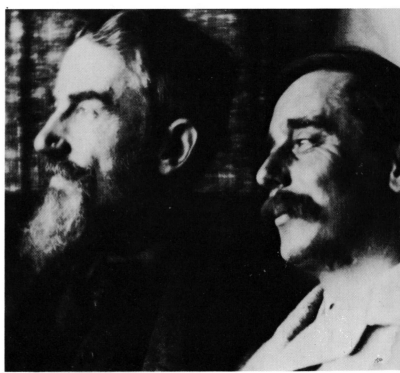

Wells & Shaw — a
struggle between the
generations

> In place of disorderly individual effort, each man
> doing what he pleases, the Socialist wants
> organised effort and a plan. And while the
> scientific man seeks to make an orderly map of the
> half-explored wilderness of fact, the Socialist
> seeks to make an orderly plan for the half-
> conceived wilderness of human effort. That and
> no other is the essential Socialist idea.
>
> **H G Wells** *New Worlds for Old* 1908

SECOND GENERATION

H G Wells' first pamphlet for the Fabian Society.

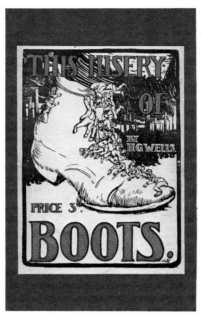

Wells exaggerated the Fabians' caution. Worse, he seduced their daughters. Ranks closed against his ideas for a massive expansion of the Society, and he was not his own best advocate. By 1908 he was gone, taking a mocking revenge with his portrait of the Webbs in *The New Machiavelli.* But his influence survived. The Fabian Nursery, forerunner of the present Young Fabians, was launched in 1907. It flourished at the universities; Cambridge recruited **Hugh Dalton**, **Rupert Brooke** and Wells' young lover **Amber Reeves**. Oxford replied with the budding Guild Socialist, **G D H Cole**. They wanted, Rupert Brooke wrote, a less dessicated approach than the Webbs, "who think that a compulsory living wage is an end, instead of a good beginning". The magazine *New Age,* edited by **Alfred Orage** with initial Fabian backing, turned into another vehicle for the irreverent young to "deprive the Society of its Webbed feet".

The Webbs, however, were stayers. They wanted an answer to the young anti-collectivists of *New Age,* a magazine which would preach the scientific socialism, disbursed by a benevolent State, which was their ideal.

The 'old guard' hit back at the presumptions - and procreation - of Wells.

PRIVATE. FOR FABLIANS ONLY.

FABLES FOR FABLIANS.

No. X.—THE FROG.

A certain frog lived in the basement of a hostelry near the Palace of Justice. From time to time he sallied forth and croaked under the windows of Cabinet Ministers, awakening them from their sleep; so that the Ministers prayed fervently, saying, 'O Lord, damn that frog!' And the frog begat eight hundred small frogs, who croaked after the manner of their parent; and, altogether, the family did pretty well, thank you.

One day the frog jumped along the Strand, and noted the size of the buildings and business places, the glare of the advertisements, the abundance of traffic and the multitude of the people, and took a casual estimate of the site-values as he jumped along. And his heart became heavy within him; and he said, 'Lo, I must *megalo*!* My poor cellar in Clement's Inn is as naught to these stately buildings; my eight hundred kiddies are but a handful to this teeming population; these site-values must be worth millions, while I can barely pay my trumpery bills for worms and water-cress! . . I must increase and multiply!'

So the frog increased by patient and persevering inhalation of air.

And busted.

MORAL.—All's Well that ends Wells.

* *Megalo*, a Greek word popularly used in Æsop's time, signifies, to swell one's head.

H. G. Wells.

LOW

THE NEW STATESMAN

Kingsley Martin of the
New Statesman with
Shaw and Cole

The *New Statesman* was born in 1913 in the Old Rectory at Liphook, the farsighted midwife being Beatrice Webb and the occasion one of her talent-spotting house parties. It was to be the national voice of Fabianism. The farsightedness enabled Mrs Webb to disregard the almost unanimous view of her attendant politicians and journalists (even, to begin with, of her cautious Sidney) that any such publication was bound to fail. She wanted **S K Ratcliffe**, of the Calcutta *Statesman,* to be its editor, but he turned it down as ill-conceived (and she never forgave him). She appointed **Clifford Sharp**, and the paper began with £5,000 put up by **Shaw, Whitley, E D Simon** and a few others, and a sale (unexpectedly large) of 2,200. By 1970 this had reached 92,000, the voice of Fabianism had become an undertone, and most of its readers would have been surprised (and probably rather pleased) to know of its origins. But throughout its editorial and other changes it served, and still serves, the Fabian intention to promote the concept of good government by the light of reason.

Clifford Sharp — Youn[g]
Fabian turned editor

The New Statesman and Nation, April 14, 1934

NEW STATESMAN RETROSPECT
on its Twenty-First birthday

CONTENTS

THE WEBBS AND THE NEW STATESMAN

It was in the summer of 1912 that Mr. and Mrs. Sidney Webb and Mr. Bernard Shaw first discussed the founding of a Fabian weekly. They were not under the illusion that the job would be easy. It was no good thinking that a paper would succeed merely because a particular set of political and economic doctrines were forcibly expounded or even because a few well-known writers had promised to be contributors. They knew that politics were not enough, and that the intelligent public to which they wished to appeal would not regularly buy a paper because there was a chance of an article by Mr. Bernard Shaw. If the paper was to establish itself

capital: £5,000 (Shaw, Whitley, Harben and Simon each £1,000 and £1,000 more in small sums), without the advice of any one who understands newspaper production. To the experienced journalist it must seem a mad adventure, and we ourselves hardly expect more than a run for other people's money and our own hard work. But then the London School of Economics did not seem much more promising, and to-day it rolls on majestically from success to success.

Christmas, 1912. *Weymouth*

Our plans for the coming year are already cut, I will not say "dried"—they are still moist with uncertainty as to detail. First there is the starting of the *New Statesman.* During the next three months we have to get, by circularisation, a large number of postal subscribers; if we can get 2,000 the success of the paper is secured; if we get only 500 it is extremely doubtful whether it can survive two years. Then Sidney and I have to contribute the long series of articles on "What is Socialism?" We have also to help Sharp to get other contributors.

Secondly, we have to complete the inquiry into the control of industry and draft the report, probably as a supplement to the *Statesman.* I don't feel anxious about this seemingly gigantic task—we could write the report now; and getting

FABIANS AT HOME.

Fabian Diablonians exorcising a mediæval Christian Saint on the occasion of the debate between Belloc and Shaw. It is not officially supposed that the Millennium will be in any way unduly delayed by this debate.

FABIAN SOCIETY.

A DEBATE on SOCIALISM will take place at Queen's Hall, Langham Place (Sole Lessees: Chappell & Co., Ltd.), W., between BERNARD SHAW & HILAIRE BELLOC, on Tuesday, January 28, 1913. Chair will be taken at 8 p.m.

SEATS:—Sofa Stalls (numbered and reserved), 10/- 5/- and 2/6. Grand Circle (numbered and reserved), 5/- and 2/6. Platform (lower rows of Orchestra, numbered and reserved), 5/- and 2/6. Balcony, Area, and Orchestra (numbered and reserved), 1/-

Please send me tickets as under:—

			£	s.	d.
....	Sofa Stalls,	10/-	:	:	
....	" "	5/-	:	:	
....	" "	2 6	:	:	
....	Grand Circle,	5/-	:	:	
....	Platform,	5/	:	:	
....	" "	2/6	:	:	
....	Grand Circle,	2 6 (ALL SOLD)...	:	:	
....	Balcony,	1/- (ALL SOLD)...	:	:	
....	Area,	1/- (ALL SOLD)...	:	:	
....	Orchestra,	1/- (ALL SOLD)...	:	:	

£ _____

I enclose POSTAL ORDER / CHEQUE for ....

Name ....

Address ....

This form when filled in to be returned to W. STEPHEN SANDERS,
Fabian Office, 3 Clement's Inn, Strand, W.C.

A classic Dyson view of the Fabian in debate. Shaw, supported by Pease and Bland (left) and the Webbs (right) mocks Belloc

LCC

Will Crooks M P

When the **London County Council** first emerged from the tangle of boards and vestries, which previously provided an inadequate democracy to the metropolis, the Fabians were in their fifth year. **Sidney Webb** published Fabian Tract No.8, *Facts for Londoners*. Its theme was clear from the Shelley quotation on its title page: "Hell is a City much like London". Its argument was a powerful case for municipal reform and local democracy. Five years later Webb and five other Fabians were elected to the LCC on the Progressive programme. **W S Sanders**, **Ramsay MacDonald** and **Will Crooks** were among London's leading Fabians. Webb himself served on the LCC for 18 years, chairing the Technical Education Board, and pushing the Progressive coalition closer to his socialist ideal.

It was only after 1925, however, that the Progressives disintegrated, leaving Labour the principal opposition. The LCC, with heavy new responsibilities for transport, housing and welfare, suffered under the cuts imposed by the National Government in 1931. The response was swift, and in 1934 the first Labour LCC took office. Twenty-five of the eighty Labour councillors and aldermen were Fabians. Chief among them was **Herbert Morrison**, "a Fabian of Fabians", canny, cautious, never forgetting his LCC base and its achievements in all his years of power across the river at Westminster. The Fabian link with local government continues. The **Greater London Council**, successor of the old LCC, was won back for Labour under the leadership of a prominent Fabian, **Andrew McIntosh**. The former Fabian General Secretary, **Lord Ponsonby**, was Chairman of the GLC from 1976 to 1977. Today's Labour alternative, expressed in local government during its national eclipse since 1979, is argued out in Fabian Tract No.491, *Building from the Bottom* by **David Blunkett** and **Geoff Green**. The spirit of *Facts for Londoners* lives on in the campaign against the destruction of local government, and all it has achieved in the last hundred years.

Herbert Morrison led Labour to victory on the L C C

LONDON SCHOOL BOARD ELECTION, 1894.
HACKNEY DIVISION.

Electors of Shoreditch (Haggerston and
Hoxton Parliamentary Divisions)

GIVE YOUR **5** VOTES TO

GRAHAM WALLAS, M.A.,

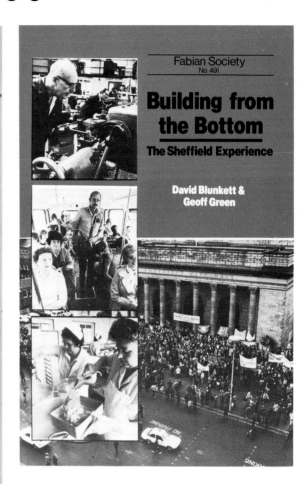

Fabian Society
No. 491

**Building from
the Bottom**
The Sheffield Experience

David Blunkett &
Geoff Green

LSE

14 The **London School of Economics** was the favourite child of the **Webbs**. It began with a suicide. The Derby Fabian **Henry Hutchinson**, who killed himself in 1894, left £10,000 to the Society for "propaganda and other purposes". The Webbs, Wallas and Shaw decided that this could be stretched to mean a research institute, a School of Economics and Political Science, to provide proof positive for the collectivist ideal. The Webbs were supported by Graham Wallas, who was offered a post at the LSE (which he declined), and opposed by Ramsay MacDonald, who was not.

The Webbs prevailed, and the LSE flourished, in association with a long line of Fabian academics from **Wallas and Laski** to **Titmuss** and **Abel-Smith**, whilst Labour leaders like **Attlee** and **Dalton** lectured there. They were honoured guests whenever they visited the LSE, and although it has never been turned into the "centre for collectivist-tempered research" which they wanted, they would approve of the intensity and international flavour which still distinguishes the products of Clare Market.

Much the same could be said of Imperial College, which owed its inception to Webb and **Haldane**. Raising money from millionaire industrialists, they constituted Imperial College as an institute of technology which could hold its own with any other in the world. In this aim, too, Webb triumphantly succeeded.

THE LONDON SCHOOL OF ECONOMICS AND POLITICAL SCIENCE.

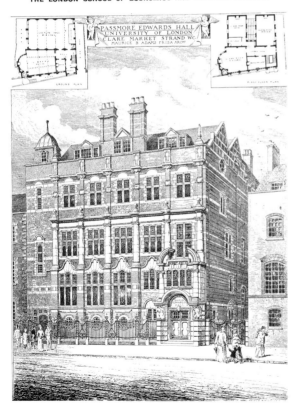

Founders of the LSE Shaw, The Webbs and Wallas

LSE Lecturers Dalton & Laski — the academic politician and the political academic

· FABIAN WOMEN ·

A century ago women, unenfranchised, no more than chattels to the law, encountered massive difficulties in achieving political and social expression. From its beginnings in 1884, the Fabian Society provided one such outlet. Its earliest members included the matchless **Annie Besant**, the writer **Edith Nesbit**, the suffragette leader **Emmeline Pankhurst**; all well before **Beatrice Webb**. These articulate and educated middle class women knew that even with their disadvantages and exclusions they were themselves privileged by comparison with the utter degradation of the working class woman.

It was not until 1908, however, when the suffrage movement accelerated and began to capture national attention, that Fabian women formed their own group within the Society. There was a big increase in women recruits to almost a third of the total membership.

Led by Mrs **Charlotte Wilson** and organised under its separate office and staff, the **Fabian Women**'s **Group** resolved to pursue two basic objectives for women: equality in citizenship and economic independence.

Its activities led to the qualification of countless women as local electors, to municipal public service reforms, and to the election of Fabian women to Poor Law Boards and local councils.

Less than typically Fabian, the Group strongly supported the activities of its militant members and formed a special committee to protest at the treatment of suffragists by prison authorities.

The distinctive contribution of the **Fabian Women**'s **Group** was its consistent and persuasive call to expand the women's movement beyond purely political demands to include issues of economic reform. In the best Fabian tradition, the Group grounded its proposals in extensive, first-hand investigations like **Maud Pember Reeve**'s *Round About a Pound a Week*, the product of a four year survey by the Group which reveals the daily lives and budgets of working class families in Lambeth. While the Labour Party (and Fabian men) argued that state-financed family allowances would lead to lower wages for working men, the Group replied that this was the only way to compensate for the unpaid labour of mothers and guarantee the health and welfare of their children.

During its forty-four year history, the **Fabian Women**'s **Group** included in its membership some of the leading women in British politics and social reform, including **Margaret Bondfield**, trade union leader and first woman Cabinet minister, **Mary MacArthur**, founder of the **National Federation of Women Workers**, Dr **Marion Phillips**, Labour Party organiser and MP, **Mabel Atkinson**, author of *The Economic Foundations of the Women's Movement*, **Susan Lawrence**, Labour Party chair, and **Emma Brooke**, the Victorian novelist whose depiction of the "new woman" foreshadowed the later works of her fellow Fabian, **Rebecca West**.

THE MODERN INQUISITION TREATMENT of POLITICAL PRISONERS UNDER A LIBERAL GOVERNMENT

ELECTORS! Put a stop to this Torture by voting against THE PRIME MINISTER

LABOUR LINKS

The Fabians had been there at the beginning, at the Farringdon Hall in 1900, of the Labour Party. Although the Webbs kept up their permeation and persuasion of Asquithian Liberalism the link with Labour was not sundered. All attempts to break the affiliation with the young Labour Party, both by those who thought it not socialist enough and those who still flirted with Liberalism, were rejected. For a while there was a modest sponsorship of Labour parliamentary candidates.

During the Great War Webb himself was elected to the Labour Party National Executive, and substantially drafted the party's programme *Labour and the New Social Order,* as well as the constitution of 1918. The research base for the party was provided by a flow of passionate pamphlets — **Leonard Woolf** on *Imperialism,* **Tawney** on the *Acquisitive Society,* **Cole** on *Guild Socialism.*

Fabians on the
Hustings — Shaw and
W S Sanders

In 1923 over twenty Fabians were elected to Parliament. Five of them were in **Ramsay MacDonald**'s Cabinet. Among the junior ministers was Major **C R Attlee** of Limehouse. At the top, this first government looked like a new party led · by old men. MacDonald, who would have behaved with the nervousness of a minority administration even if he had not presided over one, had only modest achievements to his credit when his government fell in a welter of red scares. The problems of the Twenties were to leave most Labour ministers floundering.

The Fabian Society itself needed new blood. Its response to the 1931 debacle, after which only four Fabians returned to Parliament in the Labour interest, was muted. Webb and Pease were still on the executive. But the former had only one new idea — an infatuation with the Soviet Union; the latter had none at all. The initiative was to come elsewhere. At one of those incongruous summer schools where Fabian socialists could enjoy the erratic hospitality of the royal mistress turned revolutionary, Lady Warwick, a **New Fabian Research Bureau** was born. It was the inspiration of **G D H Cole** and some of the young men he had brought into Labour politics in the wake of the General Strike: **Hugh Gaitskell**, **Evan Durbin**, **John Parker** and **Michael Stewart**. Funds were put up by supporters like **Stafford Cripps** and **Dick Mitchison**. **Attlee** became Chairman, **Gaitskell**, **Leonard Woolf** and **William Robson** took over the economic, international and political research.

The NFRB, together with **Victor Gollancz**'s Left Book Club, restored the intellectual credibility of the Labour Party in opposition. The blueprints for the future Attlee Government were prepared in these years, by the men and women who were to serve it either as ministers, like Gaitskell, Dalton and **Creech Jones**, or as civil servants of the stature of **Otto Clark** and **William Nield**. In 1938 the Bureau in effect took over the old Society in a merger. The two streams of Fabianism had come together. The Webbs, Shaw and Pease solemnly launched their successors at the **LSE**. The Coles, Gaitskell, John Parker and **Billy Hughes** took the rejuvenated Society into the War. For the Society, as for the nation, the war years proved to be life on a high plateau of achievement and aspiration, when all seemed possible, all at risk.

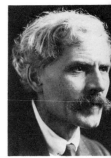

Ramsay MacDonald

R H Tawney

Leonard Woolf

The Labour Party
Conference 1906 — at
the Farringdon Hall

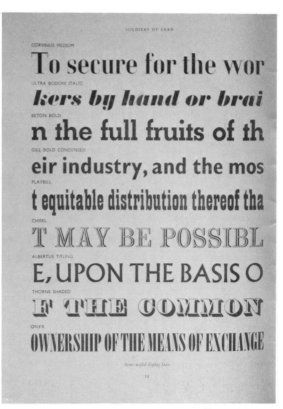

Clause IV of the
Labour Party
constitution

G D H Cole

During the darkest hours of the war the Fabians planned for reconstruction in the peace. Membership trebled between 1940 and 1946. Local societies, which remained thereafter an important part of new thinking and Fabian activity, expanded from 6 in 1939 to 120 by the end of the War. They remain to this day a source of innovation and inspiration, resilient when the parent Society becomes too obsessed with the quarrels of Westminster and Whitehall.

What did the Fabians do in the War? They exploited the popular mood that a better world had to be made, and quickly. The **Colonial Bureau**, inspired by **Rita Hinden**, attempted to set a timetable for the dismantling of imperialism. The **International Bureau** brought together, in exile, those who hoped to build a Socialist International when the War was over. At home the essays *Social Security,* edited by **William Robson**, paved the way for the **Beveridge Report**. This book, and five others, with a further nineteen research pamphlets, comprised the Fabian war effort. It was condensed in the 1945 Manifesto *Let Us Face the Future*, written by the Fabian **Michael Young**, and successful as no manifesto has ever been before or since.

FABIAN SCHOOLS

18   Much of the vigour and optimism of the young socialist movement went into improving leisure activities. The Fabian summer schools, like the Clarion cycling clubs, were typical of this. The first school was held in the summer of 1907 at Llanbedr, near Harlech. **Shaw** turned up to be lionised. There were walks, talks and Swedish drill. Lectures came in stiff doses, so that the mind could be exercised with the body. The schools became a regular feature of Fabianism, and still are.

  For forty years the annual Summer School set the scene. There was a joint school with the ILP in which the mirage of unity was glimpsed. There were rowdy scenes at Keswick on the eve of the Great War, when the young **Cole** and his guild socialists poured scorn on the **Webbs**. Sidney and Beatrice found the frivolity of the young hard to bear. Perhaps only when she discovered the Soviet Union, and reported that "there is no spooning in the public parks", did Beatrice find recreation handled as austerely as she wished. Fabian schools had their share of laughter and spooning. Unexpected stars, like **Rebecca West** and her sister **Laetitia Fairchild**, turned out in the Cabaret. **Professor Joad** was banned for staying out all night with female Fabians of tender age.

Professor Joad in full cry

The Lecture in the woods

Aylmer Maude, G B Shaw and Olivier — Founding Fabians

'I wouldn't even try to persuade you to subscribe to the **New Statesman** by making bombastic claims about how good it is. But I do think that, if you took it regularly for a few months, you would find in it a range of news, views, argument and reviews of books and the arts that would surprise you.

So I hope that you will be tempted by the following special offer. If you subscribe now to the **New Statesman** for 6 months at a special reduced introductory rate of £15, we will start you off with an extra 3 months' subscription ENTIRELY FREE.

If at any time in those first three months you decide that you do not after all want to go on getting the **New Statesman** sent to you at home, you have my cast-iron guarantee that we shall refund you your £15 immediately and without question.

So you can't lose. It's an offer of a great deal. '

Editor

Hugh Stephenson

- -

I accept your special subscription offer and enclose my cheque for £15. This buys a six month subscription plus an initial three months free of charge. If I let you know at any time in the initial three month period that I do not wish to continue receiving the **New Statesman,** you will refund my £15 immediately and without question.

(please complete this form in block capitals)

NAME: ....

ADDRESS:...

....

....

Please send this form with your remittance to:

Fabian Offer, *New Statesman,* **14/16 Farringdon Lane, London, EC1R 3AU.**

FABIAN society

If you join now you get three FREE pamphlets

At many points in its history the Labour Party has suffered through a failure to give sufficient attention to ideas and ideology. The Fabian Society has sought to remedy that failure and I welcome its contribution . . .

Neil Kinnock

The Fabian Society over the years has offered not only the opportunity for people to come together and debate the way forward for a socialist society—free from the traumas of evenings spent on 'matters arising'—but a channel for stimulating and otherwise unheard views.

David Blunkett

It's the thoughts that count

Today's Fabian Society is not geared primarily for those who think that total abstinence and a good filing system are the signposts to socialism: socialists who value culture, beauty, leisure and even frivolity should join it.

Susan Crosland

It has sometimes been felt that literary or artistic people would dilute the red blood of true socialism. The fertile history of Fabianism, with all its literary associations, stands as a contradiction to all that.

Melvyn Bragg

Membership form

Please complete and return this form to **Fabian Society, 11 Dartmouth Street, London SW1H 9BH.**

☐ I/we wish to become full/associate member(s) of the Fabian Society. (Couples may be joint members for a single subscription. Full members must be members or eligible for membership of the Labour Party.) I enclose a cheque/PO for £15.

☐ I am an OAP/full time student/apprentice/long-term unemployed (delete as appropriate) and would like to be a half-rate member. I enclose a cheque/PO for £7.50.

Name(s) _____

Address _____

Date of birth (if under 30) _____

Signed _____ Date _____

MUG SHOTS

Six commemorative mugs: cartoons of Sidney Webb, Shaw, Wells, Cole, Tawney & Crosland drawn by Reynolds, Vicky, Low, Dyson & Marc. Sold in sets of 3 at £6.50 inc. postage.

Sold in sets of 3 at £6.50 inc. postage.

BRONZE MEDAL

Depicting Shaw & the Webbs, the Fabian Tortoise and inscription "When I Strike I Strike Hard." 7cm dia.

£20 inc postage. Made to order.

POSTCARD PACK

8 quality cards

1 Walter Crane book cover design from "First Fabian Essays"

2 Fabian stained glass window in full colour

3 Annie Besant

4 Beatrice Webb

5 Margaret Cole

6 G B Shaw

7 Sidney Webb

8 Six Socialists: a drawing by H G Wells

£1.20 inc. p&p.

PLATE

9″ bone china plate with bright gold rim. The hand finished centre piece depicts the Beatrice Webb House stained glass Fabian window.

£15 inc. postage. Made to order.

FABIAN INTEREST BOOKS
FROM

Beatrice and Sidney Webb: Fabian Socialists by Lisanne Radice
£20.00 ISBN: 0 333 36183 0 hardback £8.95 ISBN: 0 333 37888 1 paperback

The Apprenticeship of Beatrice Webb by Deborah Epstein Nord
£20.00 ISBN: 0 333 36914 9 hardback

A History of Trade Unionism by Henry Pelling
£20.00 ISBN: 0 333 21330 0 hardback

A Short History of the Labour Party by Henry Pelling
£5.95 ISBN: 0 333 334736 paperback

The Labour Governments 1945-51 by Henry Pelling
£20.00 ISBN: 0 333 36356 6 hardback

The National Council for Civil Liberties by Mark Lilly
£17.50 ISBN: 0 333 36974 2 hardback £5.95 ISBN: 0 333 36975 0 paperback

Graham Wallas and the Great Society by Terrence Qualter
£12.00 ISBN: 0 333 27278 1 hardback

Socialist Thought in Imaginative Literature by Stephen Ingle
£15.00 ISBN: 0 333 24618 7 hardback

A George Orwell Companion by J R Hammond
£20.00 ISBN: 0 333 28668 5 hardback

Local Socialism by Martin Boddy and Colin Fudge
£18.00 ISBN: 0 333 35185 1 hardback £6.95 ISBN: 0 333 35187 8 paperback

Dilemmas of Change in British Politics by D T Studlar and J L Waltman
£17.50 ISBN: 0 333 36284 5 hardback £7.95 ISBN: 0 333 36285 3 paperback

The Labour Government 1974-79 by Martin Holmes
£20.00 ISBN: 0 333 36735 9 hardback

The Transition from Capitalism to Socialism by N Stephens
£15.00 ISBN: 0 333 23406 5 hardback

Dictionary of Labour Biography by J Bellamy and J Saville
Seven volumes are available all priced £25.00. Volume 7 is published this year. ISBN: 0 333 33181 8

All Macmillan Press titles can be obtained through your usual bookseller
In case of difficulty or for further information please contact Sue Berger at The Macmillan Press
Houndmills
Basingstoke
Hants RG21 2XS

Please send me:

Qty	Author	Title	Price	ISBN

Postage and Packing £1.50 per title. I enclose a cheque for £...

Please charge my credit card the amount of £...

Access ☐   Barclaycard/Visa ☐   Diners Club ☐

Account No.. Expiry ....../....../......

Signature ....

Name and Address (*please print*) ....

....

....

Longman Group

The original publishers of
"The Webbs and their Work" by Margaret Cole
continue in the tradition of publishing
key works on politics and political thought.

Recent titles include

Anthony Wright **British Socialism** 1880s-1960s
Suzanne MacGregor **The Politics of Poverty**
Professor G Ionescu **Politics and the Pursuit of Happiness**
(June 1984)
Andrew Sharp **Political Ideas in the English Civil War**
Robert Pearson **Political Thought**
Geraint Williams **Public Policy in the 19th Century**

Longman wish
the Fabian Society
success with
its exhibition

100 YEARS
OF FABIAN
SOCIALISM
·1884-1984·

FABIAN SCHOOLS

They also addressed the great issues of the day. **Shaw** and the **Webbs** continued to turn up until the Thirties, but the pace was now made by the generation whom **Cole** and **Tawney** taught and inspired. **Gaitskell**, **Durbin**, **Dick Mitchison** and **John Parker**, all of whom had worked in the **New Fabian Research Bureau**, became familiar figures at the summer schools. Some of them were held in incongruously aristocratic surroundings, at **Lady Warwick**'s **Easton Lodge**, and later at **Lord Faringdon**'s **Buscot Park**. In these, and other more spartan surroundings, the issues facing the Left, from the General Strike and the defection of MacDonald to the Popular Front and the liberation of India, were thrashed out.

After 1945, with post-war austerity forbidding foreign holidays, the demand for summer schools remained high. As habits changed, and foreign travel became easier the Fabians followed the fashion. The summer schools went on, but the emphasis switched to the uses of the long weekend and the overseas tour. The New Year School, usually held at Ruskin College, became the political focus — never more sharply than in 1981, when a packed gathering made a vain attempt collectively to will the Chairman, **Shirley Williams**, away from the abyss of defection from Labour.

A Bevanite Fabian —
Ian Mikardo at the
1952 Summer School

FABIAN SCHOOLS

The overseas schools began as early as 1911. Twenty years later a group including **Margaret Cole**, **Dalton**, and **Dick** and **Naomi Mitchison** undertook a lengthy study trip to the Soviet Union, from which they returned impressed but not as·infatuated as were the elderly Webbs. The overseas schools are now held all round the world. In the last three years Fabians have carried out two exhaustive tours of India, visited Greece, Zimbabwe, Yugoslavia and China. The tours have the advantages of the political delegation without the disadvantages of representation. Fabian tours are not regimented, and look for the different strands in a country's development, not just the official line. No other tour would leave the visitor in earnest conversation with **Mrs Gandhi** on one day, and with the **Harijans** in some remote village the next, even if they managed the holiday side as effectively.

Margaret Cole with two General Secretaries, John Parker and Bosworth Monck

Post-war austerity — George Thomas MP (later Speaker of the Commons) speaks at the Fabian South Wales School 1946

THE COLES

The **Coles** consciously saw themselves as the successors of the Webbs; another high-powered meeting of minds, the best that Oxford and Cambridge could provide. Their collaboration extended to detective stories as well as political studies. From their meeting in 1915, when she was Assistant Secretary of the **Fabian Research Department**, until Margaret died in office as the Society's President in 1980, the Coles were always identified with Fabianism. Identified with it, not inseparable from it; Cole resigned from the Society in rage at some quarrel on no fewer than four occasions.

As a couple, **G D H** and **Margaret Cole** could be like the Webbs, in the prodigious energy of the one, the imperious interrogations of the other. But there were differences. The Webbs saw little wrong with the collectivist state, even when it curtailed liberty as much as in the Soviet Union. The Coles understood the danger of totalitarianism, kept clear of the Communist Party, without ever being anti-Communist, and preached the liberating effects of **Guild Socialism**, freedom through self-government.

Their joint inspiration embraced the **New Fabian Research Bureau**, the **Dictionary of Labour Biography**, and a whole generation of Labour MPs and LCC educationalists. The prolific Douglas and the stylish Margaret wrote as well individually or with other collaborators as they did together. They were a kind of secondary **Left Book Club** all by themselves, though — fittingly — it was for **Victor Gollancz**'s publishing house that they produced *The Condition of Britain* in 1937.

From irreverent youngsters in 1914 to formidable presidents in succession from 1952-1980, the Coles left as indelible a mark on the modern Fabians as did the Webbs on their predecessors.

I am neither a Communist nor a Social Democrat, because I regard both as creeds of centralisation and bureaucracy, whereas I feel sure that a Socialist society that is to be true to its equalitarian principles of human brotherhood must rest on the widest possible diffusion of power and responsibility, so as to enlist the active participation of as many as possible of its citizens in the tasks of democratic self-government.

G D H Cole *A History of Socialist Thought* Vol.5
1960

There are three stages in the life of any woman in public life. In the first she is 'that charming and intelligent girl'; in the second she becomes 'that rather frightful woman'; and in the third she is 'that very interesting old lady'.

Margaret Cole *Growing Up into Revolution* 1949

· HIGH TIDE & AFTER ·

Attlee — a reforming
Prime Minister

When the new Parliamentary Labour Party gathered after the 1945 landslide victory many of its members had previously met only at Fabian conferences and committies. There were 229 members of the Society elected. "It looks just like an enormous Fabian School", said **John Parker**'s wife **Zena**, when she saw the PLP in conclave. Ideas followed by action, that had been the Fabian dream. Now they had a chance to put it into effect. Many of them were ministers, or administrators at home and abroad.

The foundation of the Welfare State and the National Health Service, the nationalisation programme and the independence of India; all owed something to Fabian foundations of research and argument. The pace was not fast enough for all. Progress towards the emancipation of the colonies was gradual; some thought laggardly. The pace of domestic reform slackened in the last year of the parliament. By 1949 **G D H Cole** had assembled a new group, called after Lord Faringdon's house at Buscot where it first met, to assess old mistakes and new departures. The process of regeneration had to begin again.

Regeneration came with *New Fabian Essays,* published after the Labour government had fallen. Apart from **Margaret Cole** all the contributors were parliamentarians: **Albu**, **Crossman**, **Crosland**, **Healey**, **Jenkins**, **Mikardo** and **Strachey**. The book was the first prospectus of the next Labour government. Its authors did not know that they would be more than twelve years waiting for it. The question to which the new Fabians had to address themselves, against the background of Fifties' affluence, was no longer that of the Society's first pamphlet: *Why are the Many Poor?* It was rather why were so many still so relatively poor and disadvantaged, and how did the inequalities which aggravated their condition accumulate?

For **Anthony Crosland** the preoccupation was with social equality, and greater expenditure in those areas which would produce equality of outcome, financed in part by taxation, in part by the growth rates of a more efficient economy. For **Richard Titmuss** it was the primacy of need over the demands and deals which the better-off make for themselves in the market, if its values are allowed to predominate. His younger colleagues, **Brian Abel-Smith** and **Peter Townsend**,

The desire for greater equality has been part of the inspiration of all socialist thinkers and of all socialist movements. The absence of this desire, indeed, provides the most useful of all exclusive definitions of socialism. Where there is no egalitarianism there is no socialism.

Roy Jenkins "Equality" from *New Fabian Essays* 1952

Labour's social plans
Brian Abel-Smith
fabian tract 369
SOC

CASUALTIES
OF THE
WELFARE STA

HIGH TIDE & AFTER

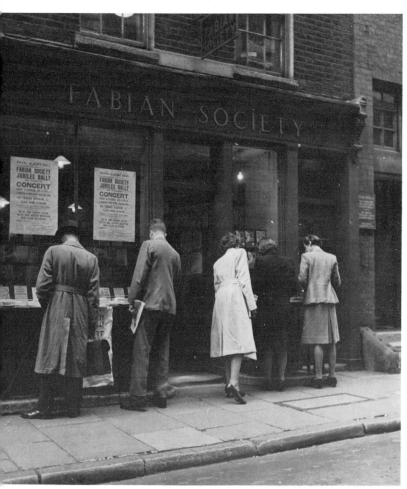

Fabian Bookshop
Dartmouth Street 1946

Class feeling, and general social malaise, still persist in England to a deplorable extent. The feeling among workers of an external and irreconcilable conflict between wages and profits, capital and labour: their feeling too of non-participation in the control of the firm for which they work, and so of non-responsibility for its well-being: the acute sense of class that goes with different accents: the knowledge that differentials in education mean differentials in opportunity — these are all signs that Britain still is, and feels itself to be, a class society.

The purpose of socialism is quite simply to eradicate this sense of class, and to create in its place a sense of common interest and equal status.

Anthony Crosland 'The Transition from Capitalism' *New Fabian Essays* 1952

R H Crossman
campaigning in 1945

began at this time a quarter century of innovative work in social policy, NHS administration, pensions policy, and the grim persistence of poverty. The Fabians identified, in the title of **Audrey Harvey**'s pamphlet, *The Casualties of the Welfare State.* It did not occur to them then, or to anyone else, that the Welfare State itself would shortly become a casualty.

Tony Benn, Fabian Chairman 1964-65

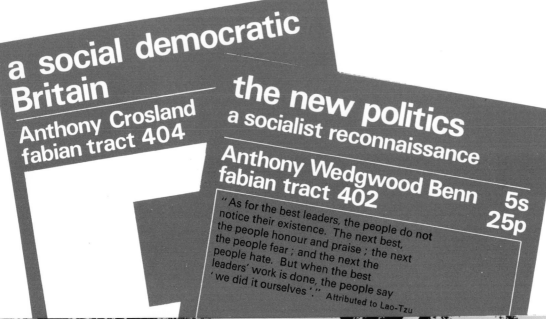

a social democratic Britain

Anthony Crosland
fabian tract 404

the new politics
a socialist reconnaissance

Anthony Wedgwood Benn
fabian tract 402

5s
25p

" As for the best leaders, the people do not notice their existence. The next best, the people honour and praise ; the next the people fear ; and the next the people hate. But when the best leaders' work is done, the people say ' we did it ourselves '." Attributed to Lao-Tzu

Wilson Cabinet 1964

· INSIDERS & OUTSIDERS ·

The post-64 Labour government leaned heavily for inspiration on Fabian thinkers, although they were not always effective when translated into office — as with **Richard Crossman**'s constitutional reforms. The Crosland belief in economic growth as the motor of progressive social change, and the sustained work on a strategy for equality based on the research of **Richard Titmuss**, **Brian Abel-Smith** and **Peter Townsend**, provided the intellectual coherence which the first **Wilson** government could have used for an ambitious reform programme. The painful reappraisal of what had gone wrong with that government and how socialists might learn from the over-optimism of the Sixties, was itself stimulated by **Tony Crosland**'s Fabian Tract *A Social Democratic Britain* and **Tony Benn**'s *The New Politics: a Socialist Renaissance.*

The Society had seen two general secretaries in succession enter Parliament for ministerial careers, **Bill Rodgers** and **Shirley Williams**, and it maintained a strong membership right across the parliamentary party. The traditional autumn lectures and summer schools were now extended with more informal seminars and overseas schools. A successful appeal was conducted to buttress its research activities. In the

Seventies this research made notable advances in the fields of alternative economic policy, poverty and inequality, industrial democracy and education. Debate was still joined without rancour by socialists of many hues. In this, by the end of the Seventies, the Society found its open house, non-sectarian approach, to be temporarily out of tune with the times.

> The chief conclusion of this report is that poverty is more extensive than is generally or officially believed and has to be understood not only as an inevitable feature of severe social inequality but also as a particular consequence of actions by the rich to preserve and enhance their wealth and so deny it to others. Control of wealth and of the institutions created by that wealth, and therefore of the terms under which it may be generated and passed on selectively or for the general good, is therefore central to any policies designed to abolish or alleviate the conditions.
>
> **Peter Townsend** *Poverty in the United Kingdom* 1979

Peter Townsend and Claus Moser flanked by two Fabian General Secretaries — Tom Ponsonby and Shirley Williams

· Tony Crosland–Reluctant Fabian ·

Susan
Crosland

Love-hate is putting it rather strongly. But certainly **Tony Crosland** was ambivalent about the Fabians. He admired their intellectual rigour and diligence. At the same time he rejected the feeling they exuded that personal fulfilment and pleasure for its own sake were far down their list of priorities, indeed, mentioned only as admonishments in the Webbs' philosophy. After pages in his comonplace book about the Webbs' achievements, he goes on to say:

"What is one, then, to make of this extraordinary pair? Their devotion and conscientious single-mindedness clearly made them v. *admirable* characters. Yet their considerable indifference to all forms of art or culture, their lack of temptation towards any of the emotional or physical pleasures of life, the consequent priggish puritanism — all this is v. unattractive and *would,* if universally influential, make the Socialist State into the dull functional nightmare which many fear."

His own contribution to Fabianism led to its approach today: efforts to reinvigorate its intellectual base are now coupled with the understanding that personal enjoyment enhances rather than diminishes the society that Fabians wish to improve.

The Society's pamphlets are influential. He used them as a vehicle for two ends: to change policy towards the aims of democratic socialism, and to re-direct the Labour Party towards the essential persuasion of the electorate. Usually with a preface about his touchstone, the people of Grimsby, he said to us: "Never forget the virtues of enjoyment and leisure. If we once appear to be lecturing people as though it is sinful to have holidays in Majorca, or colour television, or travel by car, we shall never be able to convince them that there is any point or purpose in the New Jerusalem we are trying to persuade them to build."

Susan Crosland, the writer, is the author of a best selling biography of her years with Tony Crosland

· The Heirs of Shaw – a Fabian View ·

Melvyn
Bragg

LOW

One of the things that **Shaw** did brilliantly was to take a particular subject, a flagrant injustice, and address it, not just with political force but with all the power of his art. That is how you have to see, say, *Widowers Houses.* The Fabian tradition, in Shaw and **Galsworthy**, was to cover the whole free range of ideas. Neither the theatre nor the novel do that in Britain today, for a variety of reasons. The novel treats British politics with a kind of exhausted, etiolated journalism. It doesn't address the reality of our situation. It plays games. The stage is divided between the majority of productions based on the theory that the *status quo* is really not bad, and that the past can be used to prove it, and community-based revolutionary theatre. The former reinforces liberal conservatism; no hope there. The latter, even when "taken to the people" in the streets or the pubs, is too out of touch with what the majority think, and too strident, to get through to them.

The only other political theatre we have is that group of middle class playwrights who make great statements of leftist theory, usually from the safe haven of the subsidised theatre. They haven't got through, either. Political theatre as the early Fabians understood it needs well-crafted plays addressing central issues. Today it is television which can do that. David Mercer, Dennis Potter, Ken Loach, have been political writers, allowing the free run of ideas, because television cannot be tendentious, and producing their best work about contemporary politics, which the arts had written off as being old stuff. It's not. These are real craftsmen. They have a well-made play, and they make the connection between politics and art. They haven't yet had the same collective impact — but Mercer died at 51, a fate avoided by Shaw! If the Fabians are looking today for an heir to Shaw's fusion of politics and drama they should look to television. *Boys from the Blackstuff* looks at the modern horror of unemployment in the round, lets you see the whole spectrum of reaction to it, before confronting it. It is with writers like Alan Bleasdale, not with the great names of the threatre, that we find the modern heirs of Shaw.

Melvyn Bragg, novelist and broadcaster, is a member of the Fabian Executive. The musical based on his novel *The Hired Man*, about Cumberland agricultural labourers at the turn of the century, opened in February 1984.

· FABIANISM REDISCOVERED ·

Like every other section of the Left, the Fabians shared in the trauma of the post-1979 Labour disputes. In 1981, within weeks of the New Year School, Chairman and former General Secretary **Shirley Williams** joined two of her predecessors in the first fatal step towards the formation of a breakaway party.

The Society thus faced in 1981 the defection of its Chairman, Treasurer and other Executive Committee members from the Labour Party. The rules of the Society were sufficiently ambiguous to allow defectors who still claimed to be "socialists" to assert a right to continued full membership, despite their ineligibility to be members of the Labour Party. The delicate situation, skilfully handled by General Secretary **Dianne Hayter**, was resolved by a ballot of the whole membership. It confirmed the view that the defectors could only be non-voting associate members. The link with the Labour Party was reaffirmed.

Inevitably, this decision did not please everyone, and the Society suffered a drop in membership and a spate of resignations. The crisis brought out the resilience of the Fabians, however. Generous helpers and donors replaced those who had left. Others remained despite split family or personal loyalties. A resurgence followed. There were innovatory overseas schools in India, Zimbabwe and China, establishing links which will make a richer and continuing contact with these and other countries possible.

A new General Secretary, **Ian Martin**, came to the Society with an already impressive reputation at the Joint Council for the Welfare of Immigrants. The essayists in *Future of the Welfare State,* edited by **Howard Glennerster**, strongly reasserted the Fabian research tradition maintained by **Townsend** and **Abel-Smith**.

In the election disaster of 1983 the Society was the first to shrug off defeat and provide a forum for discussion of the way back. It provided the only debate between the four Candidates for the Labour leadership, shown on the BBC. Three of the four were members of its Executive Committee. The new Leader and Deputy Leader, **Neil Kinnock** and **Roy Hattersley**, are both active in the Society. In its centenary year, with membership buoyant, the Fabian Society continues the effort it began in 1938 to construct the agenda for a new broadly-based socialism. There will be New Year and Autumn Schools on the future of socialism and on the new *Fabian Essays in Socialist Thought,* edited by **Ben Pimlott**. The centenary combines a certain piety, and a celebration of a century of achievement and persuasion, but it also allows the Society to scan the future.

Labour leadership debate

· FABIANISM REDISCOVERED ·

From where we stand now Fabian gradualism may be the only future we have

Labour faces the camera

TONIGHT the four Labour leadership candidates display their talents in a televised debate organised by the Fabian Society.

Fabians give fair hearing

By Paul Keel

THE four contestants in Labour Party leaders struggle sat on the same p form yesterday and mana to remain on their best haviour.

Fabian Society
No.489

LABOUR'S CHOICES:

**Roy Hattersley, Eric Heffer
Neil Kinnock, Peter Shore**

Raymond Plant

Equality, Markets and the State

R.H. Tawney
EQUALITY
With a New Introduction by
RICHARD M. TITMUSS
Unwin Books

C.A.R. CROSLAND
The Future of Socialism
CAPE

JOHN RAWLS
A THEORY
OF JUS

• LOOKING AHEAD •

Ian Martin —
General Secretary

A centenary is not just an occasion for assessing the past; it is the beginning of the next hundred years. And the Fabian Society has reached its centenary at a juncture which is a critical one not just for itself but for Britain and for British democratic socialism.

The 1983 election defeat has laid bare the seriousness of the Labour Party's condition, before the beginning of recovery under a new leadership. Those who call themselves Social Democrats seek with the Liberals to make permanent a challenge to Labour's position as the credible alternative to Conservative government. Conservatives have thus far escaped the consequences of a record of accelerated disaster — at the price of pervasive pessimism and cynicism about politics and the prospects of national recovery.

Today's Fabian Society has inherited valuable assets to apply in this crisis. A commitment to the importance of ideas in socialist politics, when for a time the Right not the Left has appeared to be riding a tide of intellectual support. A recognition that socialist ideas must permeate a public consciousness far beyond the Party faithful, when for a time activists have appeared to forget a broader public. A constitution which proclaims and protects a pluralism among those debating the application of the socialist values they share, when for a time socialist politics have appeared to become a battleground for sects of true believers. An integrity in the collection and analysis of evidence, when the ideologues of the new right demand leaps of faith across the unpalatable facts which belie their theories.

These assets have now to be applied to the future. Our task is not to refight elections lost but to look ahead and see how the socialist values which connect us to our tradition are to be applied in the world of the 1990's and in the next century. Perhaps the strength of the post-war social democratic consensus, to which Fabians made so substantial a contribution, also tempted their successors into the error of assuming its continuation: economic growth seemed assured, and if there were not a Labour government today there would be one again tomorrow, for which the policy briefs should be ready. Today's Fabian Society makes no easy assumptions, but prepares to face the most major of challenges.

LOOKING AHEAD

At the beginning of 1984, we are setting ourselves to rediscover the moral values of socialism and make them publicly effective again. Socialism must reclaim its identification with the fullest liberty and democracy for all citizens, and be rescued from mis-identification with bureaucracy. The language of freedom must be reclaimed from its appropriation by and for the privileged. We seek to understand not only the social change that has occurred, but the possibilities opened up by the new technology, the revolutionary implications of which for the work and leisure of men and women lie ahead. We insist that socialism must be internationalist, in a world in which the threat of nuclear war and the gulf between rich and poor are so devastating that we dare comprehend them only fleetingly.

Having taken part in the birth of the Labour Party and having recently re-asserted our affiliation to it, the Fabian Society is now part of a new mood within it. The Labour Party knows how large a task lies ahead before it can celebrate its own centenary. The task is indeed almost as great as that which faced the pioneers of the Labour movement, but we have the assets they bequeathed us to apply. Now, as before, there will be no "line", no single prescription advanced by the Fabian Society as infallible. But the Society is ideally placed to provide the research, reappraisal and argument which the Labour Party and the movement badly need. The road back for Labour will be constructed from the building blocks of reasoned argument which the first Fabians devised. In new worlds, in new ways, and in new media, the modern Fabians will follow their lead.

Roy Hattersley —
Deputy Leader of the
Labour Party

Joan Lestor

Jenny Jeger —
Centenary Year
Chairman

Tessa Blackstone —
Vice Chairman

Some of the 1984
Executive Committee

Melvyn Bragg

Peter Archer —
Q.C.,M.P.

BIBLIOGRAPHY

32 Bellamy J & Saville J — Dictionary of Labour Biography (7 vols) — Macmillan

Benn A W — Arguments for Democracy — Penguin & Cape

Benn A W — Arguments for Socialism — Penguin & Cape

Bragg M — The Hired Man — Secker & Warburg

Bragg M — A Place in England — Secker & Warburg

Bragg M — Kingdom Come — Secker & Warburg

Bragg M — Autumn Manoeuvers — Secker & Warburg

Briggs A — Victorian People — Pelican

Briggs A — A Social History of England — Weidenfeld & Nicholson

Clarke P — Liberals and Social Democrats — Cambridge

Cole G D H — Fabian Socialism — Allen & Unwin

Cole M — The Story of Fabian Socialism — Mercury Books

Cole M (ed) — The Webbs and Their Work — Longmans

Cole M — Beatrice Webb — Longmans

Crick B — George Orwell — A Life — Penguin

Crick B — In Defence of Politics — Pelican

Crosland C A R — The Future of Socialism — Jonathan Cape

Crosland C A R — The Conservative Enemy — Jonathan Cape

Crosland C A R — Socialism Now & Other Essays — Jonathan Cape

Crosland S — Tony Crosland — Coronet

Crossman R H S — Diaries (3 vols) — Jonathan Cape

Crossman R H S (ed) — New Fabian Essays, 1952 — Jonathan Cape

Fyvel T R — George Orwell, A Memoir — Hutchinson

Glennerster H (ed) — The Future of the Welfare State — Heinemann

Hammond J R — A George Orwell Companion — Macmillan

Harris K — Attlee, A Biography — Weidenfeld & Nicholson

Holmes M — The Labour Government, 1974-9 — (forthcoming) Macmillan

BIBLIOGRAPHY

Jones G S	Outcast London	Peregrine	33
Lilley M	NCCL — The First Fifty Years	Macmillan	
Lipsey D & Leonard R(ed)	Crosland's Legacy	Jonathan Cape	
MacKenzie N & J	The First Fabians	Quartet	
MacKenzie N & J	Diaries of Beatrice Webb (vols I-III)	Virago	
Marquand D	Ramsay MacDonald	Jonathan Cape	
McBriar A M	Fabian Socialism and English Politics 1884-1918	Cambridge	
Mitchison N	The Corn King & the Spring Queen	Virago	
Mitchison N	Mucking Around	Gollancz	
Muggeridge K & Adam R	Beatrice Webb — A Life	Secker & Warburg	
Orwell G	Collected Essays, Journalism & Letters (4 vols)	Penguin	
Orwell G	Inside the Whale etc	Penguin	
Orwell G	Keep the Aspidistra Flying	Penguin	
Orwell G	The Lion & the Unicorn	Penguin	
Parker J	Father of the House	RKP	
Pease E	The History of the Fabian Society, 1916 (2nd ed 1925)	Allen & Unwin	
Pelling H	History of British Trade Unionism	Pelican	
Pelling H	The Labour Governments 1945-51	(forthcoming) Macmillan	
Pimlott B	Hugh Dalton — A Life	(forthcoming) Jonathan Cape	
Pimlott B	Diaries of Hugh Dalton: Vol. I Politics Vol. II Second World War	(forthcoming) Jonathan Cape	
Pimlott B (ed)	Fabian Essays in Socialist Thought 1984	Heinemann	
Priestley J B	English Journey	Penguin	

BIBLIOGRAPHY

34	**Qualter T H**	Graham Wallas & the Great Society	Macmillan
	Radice L	Beatrice & Sidney Webb — Fabian Socialists	Macmillan
	Shaw G B (ed)	Fabian Essays in Socialism	Allen & Unwin (1931)
	Shaw G B	Intelligent Woman's Guide to Socialism	Pelican
	Tawney R H	The Acquisitive Society	Harvester
	Tawney R H	The Attack	Spokesman
	Tawney R H	Equality	Allen & Unwin
	Tawney R H	The Radical Tradition	Pelican
	Tawney R H	Religion & the Rise of Capitalism	Pelican
	Terrill R	R H Tawney and His Times, 1973	Deutsch
	Thompson E P	William Morris	Paragon
	Titmuss R	The Gift Relationship	Allen & Unwin
	Townsend P	Poverty in the United Kingdom	Pelican
	Vernon B	Ellen Wilkinson	Croom Helm
	Webb Beatrice	Our Partnership, 1948	Longman
	Webb Beatrice	My Apprenticeship, 1926	Longman
	Wells H G	Selected Short Stories	Penguin
	Wells H G	A Short History of the World	Pelican
	West Rebecca	The Essential Rebecca West	Penguin
	West Rebecca	The Young Rebecca	Virago
	Wiener M J	Between Two Worlds: The Political Thought of Graham Wallas	Clarendon
	Williams P	Diary of Hugh Gaitskell	Jonathan Cape
	Williams P	Hugh Gaitskell	Jonathan Cape
	Wilmott P & Young M	Family & Kinship in East London	Pelican
	Wilson D	Leonard Woolf A Political Biography	Hogarth
	Wright A W	G D H Cole & Socialist Democracy	Clarendon
	Wright A W	British Socialism	Longman

This booklet was prepared for the Fabian Society by
Deirdre Terrins and Phillip Whitehead, with
contributions from Melvyn Bragg, Susan Crosland,
Susan Hineley, Ian Martin, Lisanne Radice, C H Rolph
and Tony Wright

Credits for pictorial material are due to:
Humphrey Cole, Dyson, Philip Greenall, Richard
Hollis, Hubert Humphreys, Labour Party Picture
Archive, London School of Economics, Marc, Mary
Evans Picture Library, Museum of London, National
Portrait Gallery, New Statesman, Nuffield College
Archives — Fabian Collection, John Parker, Radio
Times Hulton Picture Library, Royal Academy of
Dramatic Art, Betty Vernon, Vicky, Andrew Wiard,
Workers Educational Association.

100 YEARS

OF FABIAN

SOCIALISM

· 1884-1984 ·